P. L. Perkins

THE WORD, CHURCH AND SACRAMENTS

in Protestantism and Catholicism

THE WORD, CHURCH AND SACRAMENTS

in Protestantism and Catholicism

by

Louis Bouyer, Cong. Orat.

DESCLEE COMPANY

NEW YORK · TOURNAI · PARIS · ROME 1961

Nihil obstat Carolus Davis, S.T.L.
Censor deputatus.
Imprimatur E. Morrogh Bernard,
Vic. Gen.
Westmonasterii, die 24 Decembis, 1960.

The Nihil obstat and Imprimatur are a declaration that a book or pamphlet is considered to be free from doctrinal or moral error. It is not implied that those who have granted the Nihil obstat and Imprimatur agree with the contents, opinions or statements expressed.

This book was first published in France in 1960, by Desclée de Brouwer & Cie., under the title *Parole, Église et Sacrements dans le protestantisme et le catholicisme,* and was translated into English by A. V. Littledale.

Library of Congress Catalogue Card No. 61-11030

MADE AND PRINTED IN GREAT BRITAIN

CONTENTS

PART ONE

THE WORD OF GOD

THE WORD OF GOD IN PROTESTANTISM AND CATHOLICISM

PROTESTANTISM claims to be the religion of the Bible; and it is true that nothing is so characteristic of those Protestant Churches with a real spiritual life as the importance they attach to the meditative reading of Holy Scripture. Any Catholic who wants to understand the spirituality of Protestantism must grasp this from the outset. Furthermore, this is the most ecumical approach to Protestantism; in this way we reach directly to its heart, and also to what is perhaps its most positive element in relation to the Catholic tradition. Here Catholics should have least difficulty in agreeing with what Protestants affirm about religion. Further elucidations may indeed be required not, as we shall see, in order to tone down what Protestants affirm about the Bible but solely to preserve and uphold the full value of such affirmations.

1*

I

The Bible is the starting-point of Protestantism, for the simple reason that Luther's religious insight came to him on reading the epistle to the Romans. Justification by faith, the basic doctrine of Protestantism, before it was erected into a system of thought, was first an overwhelming religious conviction that grew in Luther's soul by devout reading of the Bible. As it was at this stage, no Catholic theologian can deny its basic truth. Luther, sorely troubled about his own salvation, relying, as he had done, solely on his own efforts, his good will, his works and merits, and in despair of ever attaining it, realised in a sudden illumination while reading the Word of God that our salvation is not our own work but God's, the gift of his grace in Christ delivered up to the cross for us; so that, as St Paul says in the epistle to the Philippians, while we must work out our salvation in fear and trembling, we must also find peace in the certainty that it is God who creates in us both the will and the deed. Thus what we can and must do to be saved is simply a consequence of salvation inasmuch as it is intrinsically pure grace, a pure gift of God; by faith, by faith alone we must receive it from him as such, as St Thomas Aquinas had already emphasised; for in this matter everything comes from God, even the willing and doing of man, who has been regenerated by grace alone.

Catholic theologians may, and should, question the way Luther himself and subsequent Protestant theologians came to systematise this doctrine, which they did for a controversial end and with a therefore one-sided emphasis. But at the outset Luther's religious insight was undoubtedly a recognition, not just of one scriptural truth among others, but of the most fundamental truth of the Christian revelation, namely that it is not we who loved God first, but he who loved us, who loved us when we were far from worthy of love, who sought us out and saved us when we had deserted him. Luther, indeed, gained a wholly new insight into the Biblical teaching of the divine initiative—our God, the God of the Bible, is not just passive, letting man come to him; but he is the God who, of his own accord, has spoken to us, called to us, intervened in our life; not only has he made himself accessible to us, but in his Son made man, his living Word made flesh, he came down to our level.

So it is not enough to say that Protestantism is the religion of the Bible, in the sense that it is the religion of a book that holds all truth. It is the religion of the Bible, because it reads the Bible in the light of a living, central intuition of its content. Only in its degenerate forms, which do not express its real essence, is Protestantism reduced to the religion of a dead letter. Living Protestantism takes its life from its understanding of the Bible, not only by holding to it in a material sense, but by understanding the Bible in the light of the Spirit who gave it. Only when we acknowledge this can we understand all that the Bible means to Protestants, how it is and always will be for them a living source of genuine spirituality. In this light alone can we properly appreciate the efforts made by Protestants for the actual physical diffusion of the Bible.

The first of these efforts, and one of the most important, was the translation of the Bible into the vernacular, particularly as this was achieved in Germany and England. It is well known that Luther's translation of the Bible literally created modern German, made of it a literary language in the fullest sense, able to express the finest shades of thought and feeling. In addition, it has been absorbed for generations by all that is best in the German soul through the wonderfully vigorous and majestic expression it gives to the very words with which the Spirit inspired the prophets and the apostles, and to those uttered by Christ himself. This is perhaps even more true of England and the Authorised Version, which reproduces the sacred text with great simplicity yet unparalleled beauty, in a language more sonorous, richer even, than that of Luther's Bible. Newman, after he became a Catholic, bore eloquent witness to the singular privilege it is for a people to be familiar from childhood with the Word of God expressed in the mother-tongue, in language which by its dignity and clarity links the highest religious thought inalienably with all that is best in the native culture, and steeps therein the very genius of a people.

Indeed, versions like these are not just great works of art; or rather, they are works of art in which, as in Dante's *Divine Comedy* or Leonardo's *Last Supper*, the very depths of the human soul are set free by becoming aware of something that transcends them; and, in the case we are considering, this is the very heart of God. Consequently, these versions will always retain a spark of that living intuition of the divine Word and its meaning of which we spoke earlier, and seem to have an almost unfailing power to quicken this intuition and communicate it afresh to every reader of good will.

Yet even where Protestantism has not had the advantage of a version so excellent as the German or English, it has made Bible-reading the main basis of its public worship. Protestant services have a far greater variety of form than they have assumed in Latin countries, where practically all the churches are of the 'reformed' type. In these, public worship turns so much on the reading and expounding of the Bible that the places of worship tend to become a kind of classroom. By contrast we find, in countries of the Lutheran tradition even more than those of the English, the arrangement of the interior still unchanged from Catholic times, with the altar occupying the central place, and most of the traditional exterior forms of the Middle Ages. But everywhere, either the entire service or at least the first part of it, consists of a series of vernacular readings from Scripture, interspersed with hymns and prayers that are themselves inspired by the words of the Bible, and culminating in a sermon or homily designed to drive home the force and relevance of the Word proclaimed. Protestant worship, we may say, is basically a hearing of the Word of God in an atmosphere of faith and adoration, and this hearing is meant to arouse the response of obedience in faith, expressed in prayer that seeks to embrace the whole of life.

What then of personal devotion in Protestantism? There is a kind of print or engraving, popularised first by Durer and then by Rembrandt, which conveys the essence of Protestant piety. It shows a man or a woman with the Bible open on their knees, their hands joined, and the mind evidently completely absorbed both in what they have just read and in God whom they have thereby encountered. As if overcome by the abundance of riches it brings them by this immediate, personal meeting with God they have found there, they set the inspired book down; they want to fix their whole attention on Him who speaks in it, to whom they answer now as a child answers his father or mother . . . Direct, familiar, heart to heart intercourse with God, created, upheld, ceaselessly renewed by individual reading of the Bible, with prayer to God which is felt, above all, as a response to his own Word—this, taken as its source, seen at its living heart, is Protestant spirituality.

Behind these essential manifestations of the spiritual vitality of Protestantism we must try to reach the religious thought from which they spring. But, conversely, we can never understand the real depths of this thought if it is not first set in its native ground, in the homely reality created for it by the spirituality we have just briefly described.

Protestant theology has from time to time been accused of being somewhat anthropocentric. This is true of certain developments of Luther's central religious intuition, which reduce, or at any rate seem to reduce, the whole of religion to the single problem of man's salvation. But we must bear in mind the counterpart of this. The problem of salvation, of his own salvation, was certainly the thing that absorbed Luther before he experienced his great religious intuition; but this, when it happened, answered his problem by transposing its elements. He had been seeking how to come to God by the powers he himself had as man and as sinner, and then he discovered God coming to him in Christ, with all the fullness, unsuspected and unhoped for, of his grace. On a sudden, everything was transformed. Contemplation of God's grace, of God's love in Christ, seen by faith in the mirror of Scripture, saved the man by snatching him away from preoccupation with himself. In the divine Word resounding in his listening heart, he found a Presence that absorbed him, so that from now on he no longer tried to absorb everything in his own personal problems.

It is true that Protestantism was not to hold always to that level, and would tend from time to time, by reducing the Gospel to the single alternative of 'man's sin' or 'God's grace', to see the Word of God solely in relation to the problems of man. But with Luther, at any rate most of the time, this was not the case. 'Man's sin' simply gives occasion for a manifestation and recognition of 'God's grace', whereby the soul comes to be filled with the love, the generosity, the victorious power of Christ's grace and dominion.

Calvin made the decisive transition from the first

principle of *sola gratia* to that of *soli Deo gloria*. In other words, in the revelation of salvation the revelation of the divine glory emerges and ultimately it is this, and this alone, that comes to fill the whole perspective of the believer. The attainment of this state is precisely what constitutes for Calvin that sanctification which is the necessary counterpart of justification by faith: we can be justified by faith in the grace God has given us in his Son, in his Word made flesh, in the Word of the Cross, only by consecrating our whole life to that glory of God which is the final, complete revelation of this Word.

So it is that we come, with Karl Barth, to a theology of the divine Word which makes fully and exhaustively explicit the most profound Biblical intuitions of the Reformation.

The Word of God, Barth tells us, necessarily makes use of human words in order to reach us. But the divine Word is something quite other than words, even than those chosen by the Spirit. Fundamentally, the Word of God is an act, a divine initiative, an intervention in the course of history and of the world. By it, God challenges man, interrogates him on his whole existence. In fact, in his Word, God is not simply answering man's seeking, desire or need; but he himself is asking in his own way, which is utterly new, undreamt of by man, basic questions on our existence. But, in so doing, he is not merely obliging us to revise our whole way of looking at reality, and to approach it with a new outlook that derives from his; he changes reality itself, he transforms it utterly.

For God's Word is creative. Particularly in Christ, on

whom all Scripture is centred, his Word in the new creation. Consequently in him it discloses a new being both to us and to all things, a 'being in Christ' that we can attain only by faith in this Word. This amounts to saying that, for the believer, the true reality can now no longer be that which his senses bring him into direct contact with, that his reason enables him to apprehend. The true reality, henceforth, is that proclaimed by the sovereign Word of him who, in Christ's death and resurrection, has declared himself the Lord, in face of all the apparent might of the world and the flesh.

This can be only because the Word of God is a presence, God made manifest for us, in our world, and by that one fact bringing this world to judgment should it refuse his presence, and to salvation should it accept. For, ultimately, the Word of God is a person; it is God himself revealed in Jesus Christ, who, even as he reveals himself, yet makes us see how truly he is the hidden God, the great personal mystery that we are absolutely unable to discern, still less describe on our own, and which, even when it is revealed to us, eludes our grasp except in the prostrate but exultant adoration of faith. . . .

Reading the Bible in the spirit of faith means, strictly speaking, renewing oneself continuously in the apprehension of these great truths; for these are not truths of a static kind which man may take hold of and incorporate into some sort of conceptual system of his own devising. They are truly the shadow cast by the very Truth of God, the God of Jesus Christ, coming down to us 'the same yesterday, to-day and for ever' and laying hold of our mind and heart in that unique experience which is faith, faith in the Word of the living God.

II

Where do Catholics stand in all this? We ought openly to recognise that all these aspects of Protestant spirituality and theology concerning the Word of God contain nothing intrinsically opposed to the Catholic tradition. Indeed, they are seen to be a revival, a regeneration of that tradition after a length of time when it had become progressively obscured. We will look at the various tenets of Protestant doctrine just enumerated one by one, and see how they are, fundamentally, not a more or less heretical assemblage of innovations, but a real recovery of spiritual attitudes and theological theses that are a real part of the Church's traditional teaching.

First of all, let us take the fundamental intuition that explains and underlies all Protestant meditation on the Word of God. Leaving aside the theological systems derived from it, and therefore secondary, Luther's intuition that the basic content of the divine Word is the proclamation of gratuitous salvation, the revelation in Christ of the God who loves us and saves us without our meriting it is, beyond all doubt, in substance the message of both St Paul and St John. It is a faithful formulation of what in the synoptic Gospels appears as the 'good tidings' brought us by Christ which are, moreover, in the purest line of descent from the teachings of the prophets about God who reigns supreme, but whose infinite mercy alone can satisfy the requirements of his justice. This is the God of Amos and Isaias whose sanctity takes the expression of a justice that convicts us all of sin; but he is also the God of Osee and Ezechiel, whose love surpasses the bounds of all that seems reasonable to us, to the point of recreating in us (this is the promise of the new and eternal covenant) a heart of flesh to replace our hearts of stone, a heart on which, in the words of Jeremias, God's law will be written. And, prior to all this, he is the God of Abraham and of Moses, the God of a covenant freely entered into with man out of pure, unfathomable generosity, God the Creator who 'calls those things that are not as if they were', who destroys and recreates all things by the Word of his mouth.

Turning now to the basic structure and primary inspiration of Protestant worship, we must unhesitatingly recognise that it is basically an effort to restore Christian worship to what it was in the beginning. In fact, this act of worship which begins with the proclamation and hearing of the Word of God, in an atmosphere of prayer that is above all an act of adoring and obedient faith, is simply the first part of the Mass as it originally was. Before, forced by the circumstance of the continued use of a language grown unintelligible to the masses and, at the same time, an estrangement from the Word of God on the part of the faithful, it ceased to be an immediate and effective means of bringing God's Word to his people, the first part of the Mass had been precisely such a gradual approach to the Gospel, the 'good news of Christ' through the prophetic and apostolic teachings 'kept and pondered in the heart' of the faithful by means of the Church's living faith communicated to them. The graduated readings contained in the most ancient Masses of the Roman missal (preserved even more faithfully in the Milanese tradition), with the invitation to prayer in faith by means of the psalmic chant of the graduals and tracts, the prayer of the faithful gathered up in the sacerdotal *collectae* and, finally, the Gospel commented upon and applied to present conditions by the homily—all this, surely, is the whole content of the first half of primitive Mass, before it became gradually hieraticised by usages grown archaic, whose meaning was no longer evident, hidden by the screen of a language inaccessible to the general run of the faithful.

What about individual devotion? There is no doubt that for all the Fathers of the Church from Origen to St Augustine, the food of prayer was the Word of God, not just for an élite but for all the faithful worthy of the name. And not only in Christian antiquity but for the whole monastic tradition at least to the High Middle Ages, both for the black monks of Cluny and the white monks of Cîteaux, the only method of prayer known was what was called the *lectio divina*, that is a personal reading of the Word of God, which aimed at the assimilation of its whole substance, a reading in faith, in the spirit of prayer, in which God was believed to be actually present, speaking to the individual through the text in question, and in which the person at prayer strove to make himself present to God in a spirit of obedience and of complete abandonment to his promises and also his demands. It could well be said that this *lectio divina* was simply summed up by the Protestant Bengel in his famous injunction to both the exegete and the ordinary Christian meditating on Scripture: *te totum applica ad textum, totum textum applica ad te.*

All this we find expressed, particularly in the Fathers of the Church, in sentences as clear and uncompromising as any uttered by Protestant writers. St Jerome does not hesitate to say: *Ignoratio scripturarum ignoratio Christi est.* And for St John Crysostom, no less than Luther, familiar, intimate knowledge of St Paul's epistles was the indispensable starting-point for any real understanding of Christianity.

What, finally, are we to say of that theology of the Word of God to which Karl Barth has given one of its ablest formulations, in a synthesis of the whole Protestant experience? This conception of the Word as an act of God, who seeks out and pursues us, as a creative and recreative act in whose very outpouring we encounter the world of the new creation in Christ; this discovery of the Word as the presence of God with us, and finally as the very Person of the Incarnate Son of God—all this springs from the great patristic tradition and from the living thought of Origen and the Cappadocian Fathers, St Gregory of Nazianzen and St Basil, as much as from the best of the strictly Protestant tradition.

Should these facts surprise us, or seem paradoxical? Not in the least. It is perfectly certain that even the affirmations of Protestant theology on the unique transcendence of the Word of God as expressed in Holy Scripture are but an echo of the soundest Catholic tradition. At the very height of the Middle Ages, St Thomas Aquinas roundly affirms that the only possible basis for any doctrinal assertion is the Word of God and, moreover, the Word of God as formulated by Scripture alone under direct divine inspiration, all other sources of tradition being able solely to throw light on this one foundation but not by any means to occupy the same plane, still less to replace it.

The fact is that the basic affirmations of the Protestant Reformation on this subject, so far from amounting in themselves to a breach with tradition, are written into the very heart of a sweeping movement of return to the sources, a movement already begun in the fifteenth century and of unimpeachably orthodox origins and primary inspiration. In Italy, at the very beginning of the Renaissance, humanism, Christian in its origin in a much deeper sense than nineteenth-century historians supposed, could be defined by Giuseppe Toffanino as an attempt to recreate and revive the culture which had belonged to the Fathers of the Church, essentially Christian because it was rooted in the Bible. Ambrogio Traversari and Manetti in the enthusiasm roused by their joint rediscovery of the Fathers and of the Bible, are very characteristic of this attempt. We see the same thing later on in the Germanic countries with Reuchlin and

Erasmus, in England with John Colet and Thomas More, in Spain with the whole school of Cardinal Ximenez de Cisneros and the foundation of the university of Alcalá de Henares and in France with Clichtowe and Lefèvre of Etaples. It is quite true that historians of the last century were accustomed to designate this whole vast movement of Biblical humanism by the name 'prereformation'. If the term is used simply to indicate that the movement already showed, many generations before Luther, tendencies that he was to crystallise, and whose essential features are those we have just defined, it may be accepted without hesitation. The actual notion of reformation in itself holds nothing heretical; it is by an unceasing work of reform that the Church not only avoids altering the truth entrusted to her once and for all by Christ, but renews the living knowledge and possession that the faithful have of it. But, if we are to understand by the term that the movement of Biblical humanism, precisely because it was Biblical, prepared the way for schism and heresy, then it is completely mistaken. We see proof of this in that Erasmus never agreed to associate himself with the Protestant movement, once it had taken on these two characteristics, that St Thomas More was one of the first and most clear-sighted opponents of the Anglican schism and, above all, that the numerous Spanish bishops who had studied at Alcalá, under the inspiration of Ximenez de Cisneros, constituted at the Council of Trent the group of theologians most perceptive in their constructive opposition to the new heresies. There is another example, even more typical, that of Cardinal Cajetan, the earliest and most determined opponent of Luther when the latter had adopted doctrinal positions that placed him under the Church's censure. This, however, did not prevent Cajetan holding, more and more explicitly, that the only effective means of reforming the Church, while at the same time rooting out Protestant errors, was to redevelop, on solid foundations, the Biblical movement from which the Reformation, now grown schismatic and heretical, had originated.

III

With all these facts in mind, there is yet no doubt that the development of the Protestant Reformation very soon led only too many Catholics to look on 'Biblicism' in itself as dangerous, as the source, or at any rate the natural environment, of heresies. That those religious thinkers who had fallen away from allegiance to the traditional Church had started as the most ardent and effective promoters of the Biblical renewal undoubtedly had the sad result of diminishing, in fact of compromising for a long period, the chances in the Catholic Church of a spirituality and theology revivified by fresh recourse to the Bible. Even in Spain, where the Biblical renewal antedated by more than fifteen years the Protestant Reformation, and had been promoted by some who, subsequently, were the most persistent adversaries of its errors, we see the Inquisition going so far as to forbid any translation of the Scriptures into the vernacular, and to discountenance, to put it mildly, any direct contact of the laity with Scripture.

It is also indisputable that without going to such an extreme, wide areas of modern Catholicism came, until quite recent times, to look on direct and familiar use of Scripture for meditation and prayer as at least a strange proceeding fraught with danger, liable to open the way to all kinds of error, if not actually to lead to them directly.

In this connection it is important to note that even before the Council of Trent there were two very different tendencies present among Catholic bishops and theologians and also among spiritual writers in regard to Protestantism. The development of these tendencies can be traced in the careers of two leaders of the Catholic Church who, though they began as friends and fellow-workers, ended in tragic opposition: Caraffa, the founder of the Theatines, who became Pope Paul IV, and Pole, the English Cardinal, cousin of Henry VIII, who spent the greater part of his life in Italy before reconciling England with the Church, unhappily for so short a time, in the reign of Mary Tudor. When the Protestant Reformation had advanced and culminated in a breach of unity, Caraffa, though always a reformer in intention, came to the conclusion that the only effective way of eliminating the Protestant errors within the Church was to arrest, at least for the time, all the strivings, all the spiritual and theological movements, with which the early Protestants had been concerned. For Cardinal Pole, on the other hand, the only form of Catholic Counter-Reformation that could possibly be of any effect would be one which took over into the Church the great religious insights, the great reforming efforts the Protestants had at heart, which had aroused such a response for their movement even in the most deeply religious circles of Christendom, while at the same time ridding them of their deviations, which in any case were only accidental.

It could be said that these two attitudes persisted in the Catholic Church almost to the present time. Each of them, besides corresponding to a particular spiritual temperament, can in fact be supported by arguments that are far from negligible. For Caraffa it might well be maintained that, in view of the confusion in men's minds that very soon arose from the Lutheran movement, it was imperative to take a clear and decisive line. Once the Bible had become the watchword adopted and the standard raised by schism and heresy there could no longer be any question of Catholics using it without all sorts of safety-measures and precautions. In reply to that, men of Pole's mind might well agree that violent measures required by a state of siege could be useful or even necessary for a time, to ward off an immediate danger; but, they would add, it cannot possibly be adequate to shelve problems that arise whether we like it or not, simply because they were first resolved in a false sense. We must find a proper solution at the first possible moment; to let a given question go begging will never in the long run be enough to eliminate the inadequate response; that can be done only by the true and total answer the question calls for.

In other words, the first attitude, that of Paul IV, may be salutary as an immediate reaction of defence. But the whole truth cannot in the long run be preserved unless there is a gradual transition from the first to the second attitude. Once the false response is prevented from making headway, we must make up our minds to seek out and discover positive, balanced solutions. Yet there is no doubt that the transition from the first to the second attitude is possible only when one has managed sufficiently clearly to discern the initial error that was responsible for the false or ill-balanced response to a need which certainly had to be met. In other words, the reconciliation of Protestants and Catholics and, at a deeper level, of Protestants with the Catholic Church, on this problem of the Bible, requires not only the rebirth in the Church of a sound and vigorous Biblical movement such as we witness to-day. It is necessary, in addition, for us to discern precisely what was inadmissible in the development of the Protestant Biblical movement, what, in view of the authentic tradition, forbade the acceptance of this development as it stood. We would go further; all that we have already said on the fundamentally positive character of Protestant Biblicism binds us even more strongly, without going back on anything we have said, to bring out as clearly as possible how a movement prompted as this one was could yet come to take forms and adopt positions radically inadmissible to the Catholic

Church in the very name of the integral Christian faith of all time.

It is not to be supposed, as is sometimes said by awkward apologists for Catholicism, that Protestants are to be censured, especially on this question of the Word of God, for being too radical in the application of their principles, too strict and consistent in the development of their insights. If their principles are correct, if their insights disclose genuine truth, there can be no question of following them only half-way to their conclusions. On the contrary, what the Church holds against the Protestants is their having tried to establish their best principles on a shifting ground, their having mingled with their most luminous insights elements of obscurity which could only end by distorting them irremediably.

What then, from the Catholic standpoint, is the Protestant error concerning Scripture? It consists in having gradually separated the reading of Scripture from life in the Church of tradition, until the point is reached of setting the authority of Scripture in opposition to the authority of the Church. What was the result? It led in practice, within Protestantism itself, to men losing hold of the reality of the Word of God that they had begun by setting up above everything, and this often enough even when they continued to uphold it in principle. Protestants, when they thus oppose the authority of Scripture to the authority of the Church, none the less desire to exalt the sovereign authority of the Word of God, by refusing to let any other set a limit to it. But they thereby ignore something to which they themselves

bear witness in the best elements of their devotion to the Word of God, to wit, that the Word of God cannot remain such if the letter preserved in Scripture be divorced from the living witness of the Spirit in the Church. As we began by demonstrating, the vitality of the Biblical principle in Protestantism stems from the interpretation of the Bible in accordance with the best elements in Luther's religious insights, and these insights, if we separate their core from a shell of more or less improvised and more or less questionable theological conceptions, are in line with some of the greatest traditional insights in the Church on the subject of Scripture. But once the misconception which separated and then opposed the authority of Scripture and of the Church arose, above all once the actual rupture with the continuity of living tradition was effected, what happened? The letter of Scripture was abandoned to the entirely subjective variations of individual interpretations, and so Protestantism came to crumble into sects as hostile to each other as to the Catholic Church, disputing about texts torn from their context and isolated from Revelation as a whole, whose fundamental teachings were in danger of becoming more and more obscured through a narrow and falsifying attachment to details that were ill understood.

Later on, through an inevitable reaction against this chaos and the uncertainty it caused, a critical, historical and rational exegesis claimed to establish a truly objective understanding of the Biblical texts. But, viewing them with insufficient regard for the tradition in which they had themselves been written and then accepted by the Church, this critical exegesis came perforce to act as judge of Scripture, claiming the right to chop it up and improve upon it, to correct or at least to tone down its affirmations.

This stage once reached, what remains of the fundamental principle of the sovereignty of the Word of God? Nothing at all. Having in fact, without being aware of it, substituted for, and erroneously confounded with this sovereignty that of the individual interpretation of the text, men came openly to submit the text to the pretensions of a critical reasoning which set itself up to judge all indiscriminately, even what was most clearly outside its competence.

Consequently, the question outstanding between Protestantism and Catholicism is by no means whether the authority of the Word of God in Scripture can or cannot be limited by some other authority. It is one of determining in what actual conditions, established by God himself as the author of Scripture, their sovereign authority can effectively be upheld in practice. The experience of Protestantism and of its development is enough to convince us that no text by itself, as in any case could be foreseen, can be immune from subjective and artificial interpretations, which lead by inevitable degrees to a setting aside or diminishing, even in principle, of the authority of a Scripture that, even while calling it sovereign, men had in fact begun to distort and reduce to an empty word.

These conclusions set the problem that we shall

attempt to resolve in the next section, the problem of authority, and notably doctrinal authority in the Church, in its true context. Once again, it is not a question of knowing if we ought or ought not to add another authority to that of the Word of God, and so diminish the latter, but of knowing the conditions in which God, who inspired the Scriptures, entrusted them to the Church so that every Christian might be guaranteed against interpretations that are no better than unconscious evasions, and be assured at all times of being able to drink unimpeded at the very source of the life-giving sense embodied by the Spirit himself in the sacred text he inspired.

PART TWO

THE AUTHORITY OF THE CHURCH

THE AUTHORITY OF THE CHURCH IN PROTESTANTISM AND CATHOLICISM

THE main difficulty Protestants have with the Catholic Church (and with the separated Eastern Church as well) is on the subject of authority, and more particularly the teaching authority she claims. The opposition of those Protestants who are closest to the spirit of primitive Protestantism rests, as we have said, on the fear that whatever is conceded to the authority of the Church detracts correspondingly from the authority of the Word of God in the Bible. The opposition of those who adhere to doctrinal liberalism, however, while equally strong, has a different object, quite the reverse of the other. They object to the authority of the Church not for replacing another authority held to be divine and, as such, claiming man's exclusive and undivided submission. They object to it simply because it is authority, and therefore something inimical to the individual religious conscience.

This being the case, we may be tempted to believe that Protestantism, in the course of its development, has passed from one extreme to the other. That is to a certain extent, but not absolutely, true. The Protestantism which rejects the authority of the Church because it rejects all authority has come out of the Protestantism that rejected the authority of the Church because of the fear that it wronged that other authority, held to be sovereign, of the Scriptures. If it was possible for the first to come from the second, it must somehow have been contained therein. What actually happened?

Why did the first generation Protestants believe that they had to reject the Church's authority in order to safeguard the authority of the Word of God? In our view it was because, without being aware of it, they confused what the Word of God actually said with certain subjective interpretations, either incomplete or wholly mistaken, that they themselves gave to it. Faced with this situation, the Church had no choice but to oppose them in order to uphold the authentic and integral sense of Scripture, of which she was the responsible guardian. Consequently, the first Protestants, when they set the authority of the Word of God in opposition to the authority of the Church, were in fact ultimately opposing the Church because they refused to submit their personal opinions to a view of things that transcends the individual conscience. The later Protestants, who came to oppose the authority of the Church, not because it was *of the Church*, but simply because it was an authority, in fact did no more than take up consciously what was already implicit in the revolt, that seemed to house an entirely different inspiration, of their predecessors. None the less from time to time Protestantism has known various movements of return to its origins, whereby, alarmed at the doctrinal decay that had occurred, men strove to repossess themselves of the most positive aspects of the original Protestant positions. But then, and this is most significant, one of three things could happen. Either those who follow this course experience a genuine perception that no Christian faith is possible apart from unconditional obedience to the Word of God accepted just as it is. And then, provided they are clear-sighted enough, they sooner or later detect in Protestantism from the very beginning the ambiguity which turned a movement designed to restore the authority of the Word of God into one bent on suppressing any kind of doctrinal authority whatsoever. By this route the return to Catholicism is inevitable.

Or else in another direction, they simply arrive at a neo-lutheranism or neo-calvinism, striving to restore, as a whole immune from criticism, all the assertions of the Protestant reformers. In this case, the development which came about once, at the beginning of Protestantism, is bound to repeat itself, the same causes always producing the same effects. So it is that, just as the rationalistic Protestantism of the eighteenth century and the liberal Protestantism of the nineteenth issued from Luther and Calvin, although they would certainly have looked on them as detestable heresies, so to-day we have seen the 'demythologised' theology of Blutmann, which empties all New Testament dogmatic statements of their content, issue from the dialectical theology of Karl Barth, at least as this was formulated in its first stage, although

Barth himself strongly protests against a development he certainly had not expected from one of his earliest disciples.

Or finally, in the third case, the doctrinal 'revival' is indeed brought about by a return to the most positive of the great affirmations of the Reformers but, through indolence or inability to criticise the whole body of their teachings, men content themselves with emphasising the most luminous aspect, while leaving the rest overshadowed. The result is that, after a spiritual revival that flares up rapidly, the fervour and clarity of the initial affirmations weaken and are gradually lost. 'Revivals' that are based on certain luminous points in the doctrine but which, failing to criticise the rest, are unable to reform into a coherent whole what they have selected, drift away, one after the other, into the sands of liberalism of the rationalist or, more often, of the sentimentalist kind.

This revulsion against the authority of the Church, which so easily extends to all doctrinal authority, must not put us on the wrong track. The Protestant reformers themselves quite early saw more or less clearly that their most positive affirmations were directly threatened by the doctrinal anarchy that was in fact promoted by their revolt against the authority of the Church. In trying to mitigate this, they had a sincere desire simply to reassert the authority of Scripture, of the Word of God contained therein, against destructive individualism. But on the one hand what they ought to have upheld was not just the abstract authority of Scripture, but the authority of the truths their basic religious perception had rediscovered in it. And, on the other hand, they could in fact find no other way of upholding that authority than by restoring, more or less openly, some substitute for the traditional authority in the Catholic Church.

It is interesting to follow their attempts in this direction in some detail. As regards Luther, he very soon lapsed into a medieval conception whose mischievous results the greatest popes of the Middle Ages, like Gregory VII and Innocent III, had only too clearly demonstrated. Starting from the idea of the jurists of Theodosius's time that, since society had been converted *en bloc* to Christianity, civil and ecclesiastical society were now but a single body under different aspects, he concluded, as they did, but even more explicitly, that the head of the civil society must be considered to have the powers of a *summus episcopus*, a 'supreme bishop'. Hence the deduction that the responsibility of maintaining, by force if necessary, the authority of the Word of God—by which we are to understand, not the authority of the Bible as each one might interpret it, but as Luther himself had come to understand it—should be entrusted to him.

In the other countries won over by the reformers, such as the free cities of the Rhine valley, the outcome was a little different, inasmuch as the authority that joined with the wholly personal authority of a local theologian was not that of a prince but of elected 'magistrates' more or less directly representing public opinion.

But here too the dangers of anarchy and splintering reappeared. The unity achieved in one place was not the same as that in others; and so, in the end, there were as many Churches, as many interpretations of the Word of God, as there were independent cities, each paying allegiance to one or other of the reformers—Zwingli at Zürich, Oeculampadius at Basle, Bucer at Strasbourg, etc.

Calvin's genius lay in his understanding of the anomaly of such a situation, and its fundamental irreconcilability with the Word of God, which nonetheless it was generally desired to reinstate. It was clear, he said, that the Word of God presupposed the Church to have authority in itself, and that it could not by any means be subject to any secular power. But what sort of authority? Calvin probed the New Testament to find out, but in his examination he artificially isolated the New Testament from the whole of Christian antiquity, and brought to bear considerations which, though they were uppermost in his own mind, obviously did not correspond precisely to the situation at the origin of Christianity. He took note of how St Paul, especially according to the pastoral epistles, set over the Churches he had founded the authority of *presbyteroi*, literally *elders*, as cooperators with the apostolic authority itself. In the same way he strove, in the Churches he was able to influence, to constitute 'elders' whose main task was, in fact, to assure that the ecclesiastical organisation was according to his own views, as if he held for them the place of the Apostle. Later, when he had come to realise the fact that the episcopate made its appearance in the Church as a stable authority to succeed that of the apostles after their departure, there is no doubt that he wished to reconstitute in his Churches a kind of episcopate set over the councils of presbyters. But this remained no more than a wish.

Nevertheless, the reformed Churches that accepted the Calvinist organisation certainly regained a strong idea of the autonomy of the Church in relation to the State, to every State, and in their various councils and synods they provided themselves with an authority highly conscious of its independence of any merely human authority, while proclaiming their desire to be fully at the service of the authority of the Word of God.

This system was by no means accepted by all Protestant Churches. To many of them it looked like the setting up of a new authoritarian clericalism with no visible advantages over the old.

Particularly in England, under James I, and very soon in the colonies of New England, that new type of Protestant ecclesiastical authority which characterises the Churches known as Congregationalist developed. These kept Calvin's strong sense of the Church as the community of believers, which was therefore incapable of being in any way assimilated by the State, or even simply governed by it. But they held that authority lay in the whole local assembly of the faithful, who could not dispossess themselves of it in favour of any person. The whole assembly, in common accord, had to submit to the authority of Holy Scripture and draw from it concrete directives, day by day, for the life of the Church.

Finally, what of those few Protestant Churches which retained the episcopacy, such as the Lutheran Churches of Scandinavia and the Anglican Church? It has to be admitted that the authority of the bishops never came to be clearly defined after the breach with Rome. Either they tended to be looked on simply as high royal functionaries, whose sole duty was to apply the decisions of the *bishop* τῶν ἔξω, a title adopted by Constantine. Or else they merely exercised the function of presidents or moderators of the different councils, synods or assemblies which for their part expressed either the opinion of their Churches in the aggregate or, more often, that of a group of influential ecclesiastics and laymen.

In the light of all this, despite the repeated assertion of the *sole* authority in Protestantism belongs to Scriptures, we note three things:

(1) the first is that the authority of Scripture, if it has not turned into that of a lifeless text that each man reads in his own way is, in fact, always the authority of a particular living interpretation of Scripture—that of a great reformer like Luther or Calvin, of a great spiritual leader like Wesley, or of a powerful theologian like Barth;

(2) the second is that this authority never comes to assert itself except through the intermediary of a particular organisation of the Church, which affirms its views on Scripture and its living meaning in confessions of faith, books on the creed, and the attempts to apply

and impose these by more or less effective disciplinary measures;

(3) the third is that, from the moment men on principle reject and persist in rejecting the authority of the traditional Church as contrary to that of the Word of God, the recognition they do in fact give to the authority of the interpretation of Scripture made by one or the other great religious personality, and of one or the other organisation that strives to uphold that interpretation, are perforce no more than grudging and shamefaced. If only for this reason, the authority of the reformed Churches, at least in matters of doctrine, is as it were paralysed. Except when they are a very small sect, narrow and intolerant, nothing in all the reformed Churches to-day, among the ordinary faithful and their ministers, has been able to prevent scope being given to the greatest diversity of opinion in the interpretation of all that Scripture affirms, and even in the acceptance or rejection of Scripture itself as a religious authority.

II

How exactly does the Catholic Church approach this problem of doctrinal authority, especially in relation to the authority of the Word of God?

We begin by noting one fundamental point: if the Catholic Church claims authority, and doctrinal authority at that, it does so precisely insofar as it claims

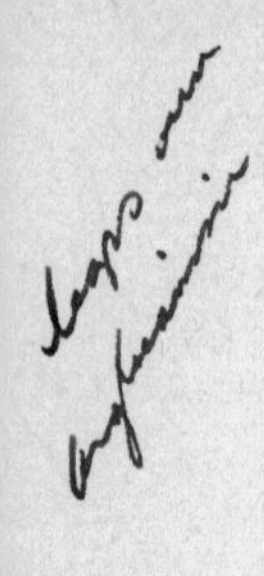

to be apostolic, that is to be none other than the very Church established by Christ on the foundation of the apostles. Consequently it is not possible to understand the authority the Catholic Church attributes to itself without first clarifying two questions: (1) What was the authority of the apostles? (2) How does the Church of to-day believe that it is linked with the apostles themselves?

On the first point, it is interesting to recall that one modern school of Protestant exegesis, headed by Anton Fridrichsen at the university of Upsala in Sweden, has established by strictly scientific studies the extent to which the primitive Church's idea of its authority coincides with that which the Catholic Church continues to claim for itself.

In the New Testament, the apostles show in the clearest possible way their consciousness of having been 'sent' by Christ, in the name of the Father himself, to speak in the name of Christ and with his authority. The 'Word of God', as presented in its final form in the New Testament, is the *kerygma*, that is the collective preaching of the apostles, recognised as the official proclamation, in the manner of the heralds of former times, of the 'good news' of salvation, the Gospel that announces that the Lord has entered upon his kingdom, and the law of this kingdom. The new covenant, the reconciliation with God in the cross of his Son—that is what the apostles are conscious of bringing to men, sent by God in Christ, with the authority of Christ himself. The Word of God in the new covenant did not begin as a written text, it was the living word of the apostles, who brought direct to their hearers not just an echo of that definitive Word of God which is Christ, but that Word itself in all truth. 'As the Father hath sent me, I also send you . . . He that despises you despises me, and he that despises me despises him that sent me'—words like this simply express the conviction of the apostles, a conviction shared by the whole primitive Church.

The fact is that the risen Christ, through the gift of the Spirit he made first of all and in a very special way to the apostles, is really present with those whom he has sent. Their authority, as a manifestation of his, is not in any way at all a legal fiction; the Spirit of Christ, and therefore Christ himself, causes them to speak and act in his name and as if in his person. 'Receive ye the Holy Ghost. Whose sins you shall forgive they are forgiven, and whose sins you shall retain they are retained . . . Whatsoever you shall bind on earth shall be bound also in heaven, and whatsoever you shall loose on earth shall be loosed also in heaven.' Indeed, these words do more than imply a teaching authority; they suppose that the Word of God in Christ is present with the apostles in all its immediacy, all its power to create and recreate. The miracles they work (the same sort of miracles as his) are the sign of this. Again, like him, they have not only the Spirit of the Father, who is also his Spirit, but are believed to possess the power of communicating him to those they will.

The French Lutheran exegete Oscar Cullmann, in his book on St Peter, goes into even further detail on the subject. In his view this power, on the one hand held by the apostles all together and collectively, is possessed by Peter personally. By the express will of the Lord, he is not only one depository among others of a power entrusted to the whole apostolate as a body. This power is his, in a unique way, and it may be that he exercises it not only together with the others, or even in the name of all the other apostles, but directly from Christ in a personal manner which immediately affects the entire apostolic community.

With some variations in detail, as Père Braun has so well indicated in his book, *Aspects nouveaux du problème de l'Église,* it is fair to say that this position is the one to which all modern Protestant exegetes at least tend, when they are acting primarily as exegetes; that is when their function as critics, philologists and historians is taking precedence over their concern to uphold theological positions inherited from their predecessors. They all come to recognise that the primitive Church acknowledged in the apostles a doctrinal authority exactly the same as that which the Catholic Church to-day claims for its hierarchy. In addition at least a fair number, if not all, of the most eminent of these exegetes even recognise, or at any rate suspect, that Peter among all the other apostles claimed an authority strikingly analogous to that which the pope to-day claims, not only over the Church in general, but even over the other bishops.

This point must be emphasised. On the other hand the most eminent representative of that Protestant theology we may call neo-liberal, the American (German by origin) theologian, Paul Tillich, calls the 'Protestant principle' *par excellence* that which asserts that the divine authority is absolutely intransmissible, incommunicable, in any conceivable fashion, to any kind of human authority whatever. If this is so, it must then be admitted that a purely objective and critical study of the New Testament leads Protestant exegetes themselves to acknowledge that the Church of the New Testament was not of the Protestant, but indeed of the Catholic, type.

What still stands in the way of Protestants who wish to be faithful to the teaching of the New Testament and prevents them from accepting the present day Catholic Church, which (as it seems) is so faithful to the type presented by the New Testament and is in this unique among its contemporaries?

Once again, it is Oscar Cullmann who has expressed this difficulty probably better than anyone. It is that they cannot see how the powers of the apostles, and in particular the special powers of St Peter, could have been handed down to others. The function of the apostles, we are told, was essentially to be founders, and even foundation stones, of the Church. As such, then, this function is intransmissible. The Church does not have to go on being founded in perpetuity. After the apostolic generation, it can only 'abide' in the doctrine of the apostles. Once they have fixed or authenticated the essence of this doctrine in the books of the New Testament, there is no further need in the Church of succeeding ages for an authority like that of the bishops and the pope, which lays claim to carrying on unchanged the authority of the apostles and of St Peter. The Church of post-apostolic times has no need of men to proclaim the definitive Word of God with the authority that belonged to Peter and the other apostles. What it needs is men who accept what Peter and the others preached and is kept for us in the New Testament.

What answer can we, from the Catholic point of view, make to this?

The first point, one which should clear up a fundamental ambiguity of this controversy, is that the Catholic Church does not maintain, and never has, that the bishops and the pope are 'other apostles', in the strict sense of the word. It teaches something quite different, that they are 'successors of the apostles'. What does this mean? There is not for one moment any question, nor has there ever been, that the bishops or even the pope may build anything at all on any foundation other than that laid by the apostles. They do not in any way assume the role of new founders, more or less independent of the first. Their role is to preserve and transmit what was communicated directly by the apostles. The faith of the Catholic Church is not something different from the faith of the apostles. The Word proclaimed by the bishops is exactly that which the apostles were the first to teach.

None the less, precisely so that this may be the case, the Catholic Church preserves this consciousness of its authority that it has always held, as far back as we can go; while not identical with the authority of the apostles, in the sense that it was meant to be another authority, like theirs but independent of it, the Church's authority is yet the same in the sense that it is in continuity with theirs (and wholly dependent on it), and is thus able to keep as alive in the Church of to-day as it was then, the Word brought by the apostles to the primitive Church.

Let us go back to what we said about the status of the Word of God in Protestantism, the status it actually holds, whatever the negative principles Protestantism clings to in its unfortunate controversy with the Catholic Church. We have put forward abundant evidence that, in Protestantism itself, the Word of God continues to live, that it remains something more than an inert text, at the mercy of any man to twist into any meaning whatever, only through the combined presence of two factors.

The first of these is a living perception of the essential content of this Word that received its highest expression in the Scriptures. The second is some kind of organism which strives, with more or less success, to pick from manifold and divergent interpretations the true one, the one truly corresponding to the intention of the divine author who inspired Scripture.

This is the only thing the Catholic Church claims when it claims authority for its tradition and hierarchy. It does not in the least deny or seek to minimise the character, definitive, established once and for all, of the teaching of the apostles as it has come down to us in the

New Testament, wherein either they, or their immediate disciples under their control, set it down in writing. But, on the one hand, it does assert that it is the very community to which the apostles communicated the Spirit of Christ so that the *kerygma* of Christ might be preserved therein, not just as a new written law, but as the living law engraved, as St Paul puts it, on the fleshly tables of our heart. And, at the same time, it does affirm that its bishops, and the pope in the first rank among them, have been established by the apostles themselves, not to do as they did and put forward a new teaching, but to continue to proclaim with the same authority that the apostles received from God in Christ *the same Gospel* and in particular to correct and rectify all the adulterations it might undergo in a community which is still human, even if the Spirit of God lives within it.

And, yet again, abundant evidence can be found in the history of the Church that just as the conviction was very soon formulated in the Church that no proclamation of any entirely new truth was to be looked for after the time of the apostles, so too was the conviction held, in perfect continuity from the Church of the apostles to that of the Fathers, thence to the medieval Church and so to the Church of modern times, that the episcopate and the papacy are a continuation of Peter and the apostles. A continuation, not in the sense of setting them aside so as to take their place, but in the sense that they have kept alive the living truth communicated by the apostles, and more particularly that they reject, by virtue of the same authority of Christ and of God that was in the apostles, all interpretations of their word which would distort its content.

In the whole course of the Church's history, and particularly in the sub-apostolic period, we cannot detect any trace of the idea that the authority which adhered originally to a living Word and a group of men responsible for conveying it should do so no longer, but should rest solely in the written Word of the Bible and in particular of the New Testament. On the contrary, in perfect sequence from the New Testament, all the texts of the Fathers of the Church support the idea that the Gospel truth is present in the Church through a living tradition which, just as it passed from the Father to Christ, his very Word, so it has been handed from Christ to the apostles, from the apostles to the bishops, and now from bishop to bishop. And the same texts are no less clear that the episcopate as a whole now believes itself responsible for keeping unchanged, alive still, proclaimed as if from the very mouth of the apostles, this same truth which in the beginning the apostles believed themselves charged with the responsibility of proclaiming to the world.

On what grounds do the bishops and the pope hold that it is they who are charged with the preservation of that truth which the apostles, and Peter in particular, first had the responsibility for proclaiming, and the authority that this implied? Our answer is simple: the Church, to-day as always, presents itself to the world with the conviction that its Master, by means of the Holy Spirit, is always with it, to make certain his promise that 'the gates of hell should not prevail against it'. More precisely, just as Peter and the apostles showed themselves to the world convinced from the outset that they had received direct from Christ divine authority for their task as founders of the Church, so the pope and the bishops show themselves from the outset convinced that they have divine authority handed down by the apostles, not, we repeat, in order to do anything new and unprecedented, but to keep intact and living, in the Church founded by the apostles, the same truth they had deposited there as a truth of life. And just as the Church of apostolic times seems never to have had the least difficulty in admitting the apostolic witness, the Church of succeeding ages, by a natural transition, without any sign of check, has never had the slightest difficulty in admitting the continuity of the episcopal with the apostolic witness.

Epis.

The fundamental affirmation that all this bears witness to is simply that the same Church continues to live by the same truth, proclaimed always to all men with the same enduring immediacy, by the authority of God in Christ, who did not merely launch the Church into history at its beginning but, through his Spirit, keeps it unshakably his own from generation to generation.

The visible basis of this witness is the undeniable historical continuity of the Catholic Church with the primitive Church. If there is any assertion that requires proof, proof that seems not easy to furnish, it is not that made by the Catholic Church. On the contrary it is the assertion, made at so late a date, so void of precedent, that with the death of the last apostle the truth of the divine Word within the Church ceased to be entrusted to a responsible body of men, invested for that purpose with the very authority of their master, ceased therefore to be the truth of a living Word kept in men's hearts, and became the wholly exterior truth of the unchanging letter of a book. Undoubtedly the first to affirm that this book, the Bible, and particularly the New Testament, bears the immediate, unique authority of the Word of God, in its determinate, inspired expression is the Church. But the Church also maintains that the authority of the sacred writings is without meaning if the truth they express ceases to be the object of a living possession, and if this living possession is not itself preserved from degeneration and alteration by the presence of Christ's mandatories who, not now to sow but to keep alive what the apostles alone could sow, have received from him, like the apostles and through them, the charism of speaking in his name and with his authority.

A point we cannot overstress is that this dual condition without which the Word of God preserved in Scripture is just a lifeless text, defenceless before the wildest interpretations, is so much in the nature of things that Protestants themselves cannot escape it. Yet what they, in the name of their own principles, do without daring to acknowledge it completely—and especially what they do on the score of individual perceptions, whose correctness there is nothing to guarantee since they are confirmed only by an authority tentatively improvised—is what the Catholic Church proclaims as the constant principle of the life of the truth within her since the time of the apostles. Her grounds for doing so is that unique continuity of life and truth in herself which is the Catholic tradition in its entirety and its unity, guaranteed and preserved by the authority of the pope and bishops, which succeeds, with similar continuity, to that of Peter and the apostles.

III

Consider now the question we have already posed: what is needed if Protestants are to recognise the wholly reasonable character of these assertions that the Church makes about herself, to recognise that, far from substituting for it some other authority, they simply serve to safeguard in its authenticity the authority of the divine Word? We would answer that what is needed, on the part of Catholics, is a great effort to make perfectly clear what we really hold, and to show that we follow the affirmations of our faith to the logical conclusions.

Now, we have to admit that only too often, theological treatises of ours written in too controversial a vein conceal rather than they clarify the real meaning of the great dogmas about the Church and her authority, and the authority of the pope and bishops in particular. In addition, our habitual conduct often does disservice to the truths we proclaim, by making it seem as if we pay lip service to them without really accepting them in practice.

On the first point, our theological writings of the last two centuries, hypnotised by the need to counter Protestant errors that, in fact, resulted from an ambiguous formulation of the sovereign authority of the Word of God, managed to arrive at expressions seemingly appropriate, but really dangerous because of the further ambiguities which they might have fostered. For example, in contrast with the Fathers of the early Church, there has been a tendency to present the Word of God in Scripture on the one hand and in the Church's tradition on the other as two distinct and complementary sources of the total Christian truth. This however is a quite untraditional idea; it is a very imperfect expression of the case, and a fruitful source of misconceptions.

First of all, the *sole* sovereign authority for the Catholic Church in questions of doctrine is the Word of God. Secondly, the Catholic Church holds too that this Word is preserved in Scripture in an entirely unique manner, since there and there alone is it expressed in formulas positively and directly inspired by God, which is not the case with even the most solemn definitions of the General Councils or the popes. Thirdly, in the Catholic Church tradition is not *something other than Holy Scripture* and added to it, but rather the entire living transmission of the truth, whose central organ is the inspired Scripture. Scripture is not illuminated or completed by tradition as by something foreign to it and superadded. On the contrary, we must insist, Scripture keeps its true and complete sense only when it remains a vital part of that living tradition of the Church in which the inspired writers actually composed it, making it as it were the essential deposit of this tradition. The Word of God is communicated to the Church and directs it through Holy Scripture, but through Scripture linked to all those things that make us see it as the deposit of a Word which is and will always be the word of life, which cannot be preserved apart from the life it itself creates and sustains.

Here is another example. Too often we speak of what we call the living *magisterium*, that is the authoritative teaching of the hierarchy centred round the pope, as if it were a new and independent source of revealed truth. It is impossible to imagine anything that would distort Catholic truth more, not only in the eyes of Protestants, but in our own as well. The *magisterium* of the hierarchy, in fact, receives no divine inspiration whatever to propose to the Church new truths. It is only 'assisted' by God, so as not to fall into error when it proposes and defines truths contained in the deposit of revelation, which has been given once and for all to the apostles and may not receive the slightest addition. Further, the bishops, whether individually or assembled in a Council, and the pope himself, in order to perceive and formulate these truths, are obliged, like anyone else and by the same means, to seek them out in Scripture as interpreted by the general sense of Tradition. The infallibility belonging to the pope when proclaiming doctrine to the universal Church, or belonging to the universal teaching of the bishops, does not even signify that all definitions, still less the ordinary proclamation of revealed truth by the *magisterium*, express this truth as well as could be desired. That depends on the piety, the theological ability and all the very various qualities, as well as the gratuitous gifts of the Spirit, that the particular pope or bishops may or may not possess. What infallibility does guarantee is only something negative: even though pope, council, or episcopal body at a given time put forward the truth of the Gospel in an inadequate manner, as may happen and indeed has happened in the past, never, so we believe, will the divine providence that watches over the Church allow them positively to alter this truth.

Finally, and this is no less important, if the responsibility of proclaiming the truth authoritatively belongs, in the Church, exclusively to the pope and the bishops, the function of witnessing to this truth may fall to any Christian moved thereto by the Holy Ghost. Among the doctors of the Church canonised as such by the Church, there are those, such as St Jerome, St Thomas Aquinas, St John of the Cross, who were not even bishops. In some cases, the most striking witness to the truth in critical times was that given by laymen like St Thomas More on the occasion of Henry VIII's schism.

What is even more important than all these considerations, if we are actually to convince Protestants that the Catholic statements on the authority of the Church, far from diminishing the sovereign authority of the Word of God simply aim at making it effective, is the practical effort we make to know this Word. It is by making it our spiritual sustenance, by scrutinising the Scriptures in the light of tradition as a whole, in a spirit of docility to the teachings of the hierarchy, that we will bear witness that this is the only way the Word of God can in all its truth shine in men's hearts free from adulteration, driving out all the darkness of error, so as to become for the whole world the source of true life, the life of God spread, together with his love, into our hearts by the Holy Ghost.

PART THREE

THE SACRAMENTS

THE SACRAMENTS IN PROTESTANTISM AND CATHOLICISM

It seems to me that the uncertainty inherent in Protestantism is nowhere so pronounced as in the sphere of the sacraments. The great Protestant Churches have all retained baptism and the Eucharist as sacraments formally recognised as such. The Lutheran Church has also kept, to-day in principle, but for a long time in the past in fact, penance as a kind of third sacrament of a private nature. Moreover, without calling them sacraments, these Churches all possess an ordination or solemn consecration of their ministers by the laying on of hands. They solemnise the celebration of Christian marriage. Finally, they all have, whether they call it confirmation or by some other name, a ceremony marking the fulfilment of Christian initiation. It is only the anointing of the sick that has left no trace in Protestantism, although at various times there have been attempts, especially in the anglo-saxon countries, to reintroduce something equivalent.

Yet if we ask why they perform these different rites, what use they have, the answers given seem as a general rule forced and somewhat embarrassed. As regards baptism and the Eucharist, they entrench themselves behind the express command of Our Lord. But as they understand it the purpose of what he prescribed does not seem very clear.

The traditionalist Lutheran Churches are fairly sharply separated on this point from the other Protestant Churches. In reality, they remain basically, even though incompletely, Catholic in their attitude towards baptism and, as they continue to call it, the sacrament of the altar. In their belief in the mysterious efficacity of baptism to bring the grace of regeneration, and in the real presence of the true body and blood of Christ under the sacred species, true Lutherans assign, at least to these sacraments, the place in the interior life that they have with Catholics. The only remark we might make, particularly in connection with the Eucharistic Supper (which, however, they continue to call the Mass in countries long Lutheran) is the almost exclusive focusing of their devotion on the individual gift offered to the believer. But we must not forget that it was the same with all good Catholics too at the end of the Middle Ages . . . and how many are there who have never gone beyond this narrow point of view, even among the most devout?

None the less, Lutheranism, even more so than Anglicanism, represents in this matter what is clearly a survival. This is not where the real Protestant problem of the sacraments makes its appearance. Let us take instead baptism in the reformed Church of France or Switzerland.

The whole liturgy is just a collection of pious exhortations and long prayers in which it is above all a question of presenting the child to the Church, of bringing out the religious and moral responsibilities of people towards the child. In the end it does indeed come to the essential rite, but despite the reading of the scriptural passages which recall the institution of the sacrament, it leaves the impression of being rather slurred over. Why this archaic gesture, this pouring of water, these sacred words? It is all absolutely without connection with what went before, and it is clear that there is very little notion of what meaning is to be ascribed to it. It is done because Christ ordered it but, once again, it is not really seen why he wished it to be done, and so there is a rather uneasy feeling about the matter.

The same kind of thing happens with the Eucharist. In those Protestant Churches which do not try to imitate the Catholic Church, it is celebrated only rarely, three or four times a year, and only before a small group of the devoted faithful after the greater number of the parishioners have left the Church on the conclusion of the service strictly so-called. Here again, and even more than in the case of baptism, in the ancient reformed liturgies the ceremony wanders around the rite at great length, as if in some doubt what is meant. The faithful are vigorously warned against the danger of attaching too much importance to it, 'as if Our Lord were materially enclosed there', they are told. And then there is a change of tone: 'We are not to think, however, that the Holy Supper is a vain and ineffectual ceremony'. But, in

ooh!

that case, what exactly does it signify, what is its aim? We will be told, once again, that this is not precisely known. It is highly characteristic that the pastor, when giving each person the bread or the chalice, pronounces a different verse of Scripture which he tries to adapt to the individual case, when he knows the person. This verse becomes, for the devout, the thing they hold on to, as if to fill the void of the sacrament itself. . . .

This being so, it is not very surprising that many Protestants, even the very devout and sincere, never or hardly ever communicate. Communion, they say, brings them no benefit, and in any case they do not see the need for it.

How have Protestants come to this way of thinking? It seems to me that there are two reasons. One is an instinctive repugnance based on certain misunderstandings, themselves arising from what were certainly abuses in medieval Catholic practice. The other is a doctrine that is correct, even very fine, basically, but is understood in a manner harsh, narrow, and ultimately quite barren. First of all, Protestantism scents magic in everything sacramental. Within this prejudice of theirs can be discerned two quite distinct zones. There is, firstly, the survival and the exaggeration of an Augustinian tendency, more or less Platonist, which was already pronounced all through the Middle Ages, but predominated without counterbalance in the reformed Churches. This was the tendency to reduce the spiritual to the interior life, to look on all that is corporeal or sensible in religion as, at best, superfluous and of dubious value. The more a person discards intermediaries of this kind, it was thought, the more 'spiritual' he becomes. We have read of those ascetics who, since they could not avoid having a body, got on with it as best they could, which was rather badly at that. The Protestants generally looked askance at all asceticism, which they suspected of being an attempt on the part of man to gain salvation by his own merits. But they were instinctively in complete agreement with the ascetics, even with the strictest among them, in despising the body and viewing with suspicion any part it might play in the spiritual life.

The Quakers, who have no rites at all, no external worship, are not, strictly speaking, Protestants and Protestants in general do not venture to go as far as they. But they are certainly in the instinctive line of Protestantism, and the most devout Protestants always look to them with something like envy.

It may be noticed that this tendency to a spiritualism carried to such lengths is very strange among people so enamoured of the Bible. The Bible itself is far from being spiritual in that sense. No doubt, it demands 'worship in spirit and in truth', but this has never meant a worship which fears or revolts from all external manifestations or aids, but one which comes from the heart, in which there dominates the influence of the Spirit of God over our spirit open to the 'truth', that is to say the true reality, concerning both us and God, through the teaching of Christ. For the majority of Protestants, on the contrary, this formula, torn forcibly from its context in

St John's Gospel, means no more than worship without formulas and rites.

Where, then, did Protestants come by their attachment to this spiritualism of theirs, so unscriptural in its basis? There is no doubt that it derives from the fact that Protestantism was born in a reaction against forms of devotion undoubtedly grown materialistic. In this respect, Protestantism has merely carried to the extreme a reaction already initiated at the close of the Middle Ages by 'spirituals', themselves encouraged thereto by the Augustinian tradition.

It is quite idle to try and disguise the fact that, among the masses and even in the religious Orders, devotion at the end of the Middle Ages seems to have been too often a simple matter of external practices, which people multiplied without much concern about their meaning. Abuses connected with the trade in indulgences, others bound up with the offering of the Mass for a determined object, the habit of making use of rites in ignorance or total incomprehension of the meaning of the liturgical prayers accompanying them and, added to all this, an abundance of practices and ideas obviously superstitious—all this naturally gave a great part, at least, of the ritual and especially the sacramental life the unfortunate appearance of a kind of magic more or less lucrative for the clergy.

Luther's treatise *De captivitate babylonica* shows clearly how, for someone craving true spirituality, the whole ritual and sacramental side of the liturgical life of the time seemed a kind of monstrous machinery set in motion for an ignorant people by avaricious priests, which claimed to dispense the grace of God and to mint it at will. Further, the unfortunate language of the decadent theology of the time often lent itself to this interpretation, giving the impression that the efficacity of the rites was of much the same kind as that of the formulas and imprecations used by sorcerers.

Here, by contrast with what we said before, it must be acknowledged that a purely scriptural influence ranged the first Protestants against any conception of religion that as it were imprisoned God, enclosed him in a ritualistic system, thereby putting him at the disposal of priests who were thus enabled to dispense his graces as it suited them, in return for payment. If there is one thing against which all the prophets of the Old Testament constantly inveigh, it is precisely that. God, the God of heaven, is the sovereign God, whom no man can bind by sacrifices but who, on the contrary, freely reveals himself out of love, gives himself to those who did not know him; he is to be received no otherwise than in adoring faith. Most unfortunate, it must be admitted, was a representation of the sacrifice of the Mass only too prevalent in late medieval theology, which envisaged it as primarily an action of the Church exercised on God to promote and increase the pouring down of his benefits on men. Quite certainly, the theologians who expressed themselves in this way were well aware that the sacrifice of the Mass exists only through the free gift God made us in Christ, and therefore is itself preeminently a grace, and by no means a lever placed in man's hands to constrain God in some way or other to benefit us. But formulas of this kind were only too likely to give the ordinary people a purely magical idea of the Eucharist.

In a more restricted field, Protestant opposition came to be centred, and since then always has been, on a particular way of understanding the *opus operatum*. Catholic theologians distinguish those sacred actions which are efficacious through the act of the person performing them, the fervour of his prayer, his personal holiness; these are said to be efficacious *ex opere operantis,* in virtue of the work or the effort of the person acting. In contrast to these pious works, which remain essentially our own, the sacraments act not in virtue of any merit of ours, neither of the celebrant nor of the ordinary faithful, but in virtue solely of the grace of God, who has given them to be for us signs, efficacious signs, of his love. We say, then, that the sacraments act *ex opere operato,* by themselves, which means that even in our hands they remain the work not of us but of God. Rightly understood, then, *opus operatum* means precisely that the sacrament is grace, the gift of God, beyond the power of man. But, badly explained and wrongly understood, the contrary idea can well be entertained of an action that acts through itself, not only apart from the personal sentiments of the priest who posits it, but apart from God's own free and gratuitous initiative; as if, in the sacrament, man had found a 'trick' to compel God to act as we want.

This way of looking at the matter is a complete caricature. It amounts to making a formula assume the exact opposite of its true meaning. Yet there is no misinterpretation, no tragic misconception of the meaning of Catholic doctrine, to which Protestants seem so closely and irrevocably attached as this. Herein lies the root of their opposition to Catholic sacramentalism, and of their own distrust of all sacramentalism.

Can we at least reassure and console ourselves by saying that this caricature is entirely due to Protestants looking at our practices from the outside, without really entering into the spirit of our theology? That, however, would be too simple and easy an explanation. We must not forget that the first Protestants had begun by being Catholics and, generally, desired to be fervent ones. What they fought against were errors and deformities which they were fully conscious of having once shared. Even to-day, despite all the progress made since the sixteenth century, can we deny that there is only too often, in our sacramental practice, superstition in disguise? Many Catholics, even the very devout, would seem to think that holiness for them was in direct proportion to the number of their Communions, even if they make no personal effort to receive the sacrament with fervour. And how many Catholics are there who have Masses said to obtain, come what may, something they are anxious for, even if its moral goodness is at least doubtful, and who expect therefrom a quasi-automatic result as if from some magical practice; in fact, they are doing well if they do not combine Christian practices with purely pagan ones, such as carrying lucky charms and the like.

At the same time, the utterances of our popular preachers and even of theologians engaged too much in countering error and not enough in keeping the balance characteristic of traditional theology, seem at times to forget that God is at all times the sole master of his gifts; that neither by the sacraments nor by any other means can we, strictly speaking, act on him, still less constrain him in any way to do what he would not otherwise do.

II

Protestantism, however, was not to rest content simply with rejecting these disastrous corruptions or deformities of doctrine. It strove to arrive at its own positive doctrine on the sacraments. This, it must be admitted, has some excellent features which could have been the starting-point of true revival. Unfortunately, they proved to be incapable of full development; in fact, they too at times were so narrowed down as to acquire a meaning quite the opposite of the original intention.

We will look first at the reformer who on many points held the most thoroughly negative doctrine on the sacraments, Ulrich Zwingli, of Zürich. In opposition to Luther himself, he came to deny completely any kind of real presence of Christ in the sacrament of the altar. Yet it would be quite mistaken to confine our attention exclusively to this aspect of his teaching. He was, in fact, one of the first modern Christians to have reacted strongly against the tendency to a wholly individualistic view of the sacraments, which came to the fore at the end of the Middle Ages and was carried to the extreme in Lutheranism. For Zwingli, on the other hand, the sacraments were intended to serve not so much the individual Christian as the people of God as a whole. To put it more precisely, by the celebration of the sacraments, and especially of the Eucharist, the people of God becomes conscious of itself as a distinct people, conscious of its spiritual unity. From this point of view, the Eucharistic Supper is a feast, the feast of the Church gathered together in common faith in the resurrection of Him who was dead, and who is now 'the one living for ever'.

It is quite certain that, while not expressing themselves so exactly, the various reformers, even Luther, despite the individualism we have pointed out, and above all Calvin, all reaffirmed at least something of the essentially corporate character of the sacraments that had become so obscured at the end of the Middle Ages. Even in the total suppression of so-called private Masses,[1] we must recognise the quite correct perception on the part of the first Protestants that the Eucharist is an essentially public act, an act of the whole Church, which ought to be present and to take part in it in all its members, as far as possible.

We know that in the Middle Ages the reception of Communion by the laity had become so infrequent as

[1] The term *Missa Privata* has just been abolished by the new liturgical prescriptions from Rome (translator).

to seem an exceptional occurrence. We do not always realise that the practice in many of the reformed Churches of celebrating the Eucharistic Supper only three or four times a year is only a consequence of the practice prevalent well before the Reformation of communicating equally seldom. Already in the fifteenth century a move back to frequent Communion can be seen; but it has not always been noticed to what extent Calvin shared it. For him, the Eucharist could not be celebrated except publicly, but it had to be celebrated every Sunday, at least in every parish, and as many as possible of the faithful were to be summoned to take part in it regularly. As it happened, this was one of the parts of Calvin's work which came up against a trend already present in the reformed Churches, and which came to exert a wide influence only in quite modern times. In this respect Calvin's work, particularly in the way it was to develop, led not towards a steady divergence from Catholicism, but to an effort, for a long time unsuccessful, to recover certain elements of the true Catholic tradition which, after they had begun to decay in medieval Catholicism, had early been rejected by Protestants.

However, the most original element of the sacramental teaching of the reformers is not to be found here. It consists, rather, in a Lutheran doctrine directly inspired by St Augustine, but whose implications were fully brought out only by Calvin. I refer to the fundamental idea that the sacraments must be seen in conjunction with the Word of God, and, more particularly, that they are in the nature of a visible word, *verbum visibile.*

In this connection, we recall what was said in the first section about the importance of the Word of God, and what it meant in early Protestantism.

For both Luther and Calvin, the Word of God does not consist simply in the letter, however inspired. It is an event, God's intervention in our life; it does not merely illuminate by the teaching it brings, but transforms by the creative power of the Word he proclaims to us.

To say, then, that the sacrament is a visible Word must mean that it is a mysterious event in which the Word touches us directly, not only to enlighten us but to act within us, to change our whole life by bringing to it the life of Christ himself.

This is, indeed, the purport of the best elements in the teaching of Luther and also of Calvin. Still it must be said that neither of these, still less their successors, give the impression of having fully worked out all the implications.

Indeed they certainly seem in this connection to have allowed themselves to be cramped by the arid intellectualism of the late Middle Ages. As a result, their assertion that the sacrament is a *verbum Dei visibile* too easily came to be understood to mean that it is a kind of inferior Word, good for simple people, for those unable to read, or those whose mentality was too crude to be able to profit easily and directly from a more abstract form of teaching. In other words, the sacrament, a visible Word, tended to be thought of as the same sort of thing the imagery of the cathedrals was for ordinary people. There was no understanding that it brings anything which the spoken Word, by itself, has not already brought, and brought much better, at any rate to those capable of hearing it.

This point is most important. Here we meet, in the first Protestants, carried one step further, that gradual deterioration of the sacramental idea itself that we have already seen in medieval devotion. The *Expositiones Missae* of the late thirteenth and fourteenth centuries explain the Mass as a sort of pious drama, in which Christ's Passion is present because mimed in a more or less evident fashion. The reading of the epistle at the right-hand side, it is said, is Christ before Pilate; that of the Gospel at the left, Christ before Herod; the *lavabo,* Pilate's washing his hands. This absolute travesty of the real meaning of the liturgy of the Mass undoubtedly led to the reduction of the whole sacramental mystery to an artificial symbolism, which merely expressed in visible imagery what was taught by word of mouth.

Furthermore, the degradation within Protestantism of the essence and reality of the sacrament points to a degradation, at least in prospect, of the Word itself. For, however strongly Luther asserted the power of the divine Word, which of itself effects what it proclaims, by its own power, he does not always see what this involves. Calvin himself, who repeats what Luther says, shows a still stronger tendency to understand it in an exaggeratedly intellectual sense. How, according to him, does the Word act in us? Simply by the psychological effect that the understanding of its meaning has on us. Likewise, there is no presence of Christ in the sacramental elements but, in receiving the sacrament, the mind of the Christian is lifted up to heaven where Christ, whom it brings to his mind, gives himself to him.

All this is manifested in the marked tendency of all the reformed Churches virtually to let the holy table be overshadowed by the pulpit, so that the Church becomes merely a lecture-hall. It is undeniable that the celebration of the sacrament has come to seem somewhat incongruous in Protestant Churches, since a too intellectualist conception of the Word, to say nothing of the sacrament itself, has reduced them to being simply schools of religious instruction. Here it is not simply an artificial 'spiritualism' that has caused this aridity, but also a distillation into mere concepts of the living reality of Christianity; and this paved the way for its rationalisation in the following centuries.

III

To draw attention to this deficiency is perhaps the best way to help a recovery by Protestantism, along the best lines of its spirituality and its theology, of the true meaning of the Catholic doctrine of the sacraments and so of their real nature; it is this that Protestantism seems to be groping after and not yet to have found.

Here let us recall what we said about the Word as understood by the best Protestant tradition, which is in line both with the greatest of the Fathers of the Church and the undeniable teaching of the Bible.

The Word of God is an act, an act of God, a truly creative act. God has but to speak to act, to create; and this presupposes that the Word of God is God present, God coming to us and, ultimately, that it is God himself revealing himself to us in his Son, his eternal Word who took flesh to redeem us. That means that the supreme Word of God to men is Christ, and not only all he said, but all he did (and particularly his cross, with all its consequences), and finally all that he is for ever in his state of being risen, glorified, triumphant over death, and establishing us for ever with himself in the divine life, the life of the Spirit given to us.

If this is so, it must be obvious that the Word of God the Church has to bring to the world cannot be merely a kind of instruction. Nor can its highest expression be found in teaching, in preaching, as if all that came after merely repeated, on a lower plane, what was already said more exactly by purely oral and intelligible means. The Word that is simply listened to, since it is the Word of God such as we have described, tends of itself to become an event, an event of our life in which the divine life encounters and possesses it. This divine fact, which comes to meet us by taking into itself our own personal acts, is precisely what, according to the teaching and practice of the Catholic Church, the sacrament is, and this is perfectly in accord with the teachings of St Paul and St John.

A man is immersed in water and comes out cleansed and as if renewed. The Word of God takes hold of this action and inserts into it the reality of a death and resurrection with Christ, of a new birth which is a birth from above, a birth of water and the Spirit.

The baptised assemble together. One of them—whom Christ has sent for the purpose, whom he has made his depository of power, in some way, as regards all the rest—takes the bread of our ordinary sustenance, the cup of our wine and does again with them at Christ's command and in his name, what he himself had done, saying again his own words, 'This is my body, this is my blood . . .'; all believe that henceforth 'as often as we eat this bread and drink this chalice, we show the death of the Lord until he come, . . . for the bread that we break is the partaking in his body, and the chalice of benediction which we bless is the communion of his blood'. So, 'we being many, are one bread, one body, all that partake of one bread'; we are the very body of Jesus Christ dead and risen.

What, then, is it which works this wonderful thing, the reality of which remains veiled under signs and is perceptible only to the faith which takes hold of the divine Word? Precisely the power of the divine Word, proclaimed by those he sent for the purpose as if he himself were speaking again in them; and it is, indeed, he who in them speaks to us by them, but always factually and directly. It is not our merits or prayers, nor even our faith, in so far as all these are from us—nor those of the faithful or the officiating priest—that is able to bring about such an effect. God alone can do so, God who spoke once and for all in Christ, in Christ who continues to speak in his apostles and the apostolic Church, their continuation. In this way, the sacrament derives all its virtue from the divine Word, the Word which instituted it during Christ's life on earth, the Word which Christ handed on to his apostles, and after them to the ministers who succeeded them; so that when they speak in his name, repeating what he said, it is always, to the eye of faith, he who is speaking and who, speaking as he did in time past, does again what he did then by his words.

Consequently, the consecrating power of the words used at the institution of the Eucharist does not derive from their being a magical formula, a trick found or devised by man to conjure up a miracle at will. It comes wholly from the fact that God in Christ, through the apostles whom Christ sent and through their successors, is always present in his Church, the same yesterday, to-day and to-morrow. Since he speaks through them, in them, then by uttering the decisive words by which Christ delivered himself up to the Father and gave himself to the world on the cross, the body of Christ crucified, the blood of his love shed for our sins are made present under the signs that he chose, and the mystery of Christ is not only announced to us for our understanding, but made open, communicated for us to enter into it, for it to become our mystery—'Christ in you the hope of glory', as St Paul says.

All this is comprehensible and possible only if it is fully understood that the Word of God cannot consist merely in something written, but is primarily a living Word. It is a living Word of which it is not enough to say that it is entrusted to the Church; its presence, ever active through the ages, being the presence of Christ himself, is what constitutes the Church. This presence is perpetuated in and through those he has chosen as his ministers precisely so that they will speak in his name in every place and through all generations, promising to give his Word as spoken by them the same virtue as it had when uttered by him. For in those he has sent, it is always he who is present, who speaks and acts, so as to keep always present, ever active, his mystery, the mystery of his cross and resurrection, the mystery of the Church and of his gift to it and for it, the mystery which is, so to speak, the final word the Word of God had to speak to us.

* * *

Now that we have reached this point, we shall briefly sum up the essence of all that has been said and bring it to a conclusion.

It is of the first importance to emphasise the last point we have made, namely that the divine Word has its culmination in Mystery. Mystery, in the Christian sense, the sense given particularly by St Paul, is not some unintelligible reality or other. It is the reality that makes up the basis, the entirety, the unity of our faith. It is the reality to which all the preparations, all the long and patient explanations of the divine Word lead, but which once present, once given, goes beyond all explanations, all that belongs merely to the sphere of ideas or reasoning and issues in the living reality, the supremely personal reality of a divine Presence, of a gift of self that God made man accomplished on the cross and never ceases to communicate to us by the inexhaustible virtue of the cross. 'Jesus Christ and him crucified', as St Paul said to the Corinthians, is then the first Word, and the last, of the Church's preaching to the world.

But preaching Christ crucified would have no significance unless Christ were present in those he has sent to preach him and, by means of this preaching, this proclamation, this *kerygma*, to communicate him, give him to the world so that the world may in some way return into him and be recreated.

So the authority of the Church, its teaching authority, is not given it by Christ simply in order to keep intact, always correct, a revelation that is merely a transmission of ideas. The authority of the Church is simply the first result of the presence in the Church of him whose intention is not just to be with it all days to the end of the world, but to communicate himself through it, actually and immediately, to people of all times and places, to reconcile them all in his Body, with each other and with the Father.

For this unity to be fully realised, we do not ask our separated brethren to forego any part of what is positive and authentic in their great religious insights. On the contrary, we ask them to draw from these fearlessly all their logical conclusions. We ask them to realise that the Church does not oppose them in order to deny or to minimise what they rightly hold to be essential, but rather to safeguard the full reality, in a completeness that no truth of Christianity can possess except in the one, whole body of Christ.

None the less, to have the right to ask of them this effort, we Catholics have to make one of our own, which undoubtedly is no less considerable and urgent than that we require of them.

We must, in the first place, understand them and, before hastening to say 'no' to what is erroneous, however extensive, be prompt to say 'yes', frankly and unreservedly, to all truths, even and especially if they are ones to which we habitually pay little attention. Afterwards, no doubt, but only afterwards, comes the corresponding duty to help our brethren to sort out for themselves the great truths they have rediscovered from the errors involved with them. This second task, certainly, is no less essential to a real 'ecumenicism' than the first; but to enter on it without regard for the first, without working at the first, would be to toil in vain.

This being so, it is equally essential for us to give a clear, positive witness to the truth that we chance, or rather have the undeserved grace, to possess. But this witness must be given to the *whole* truth, and not merely to certain aspects of it to which we habitually restrict ourselves out of habit, facility or mere indolence. Since there is but one Christian truth, Catholic truth in the real sense of the word, that is, a truth complete and whole, it is by making this effort of total fidelity to our own patrimony, and making it fully, that we shall be best prepared to make the required effort of opening our minds to the truths rightly cherished by our separated brethren.

But we must be fully aware that all that has been said will be of no effect unless accompanied by an effort, constantly renewed, to bring our own practice, our daily life, into harmony with the doctrine we profess.

We have already stressed how the controversy between Protestants and Catholics on the subject of the sacraments comes to a deadlock over the problem of the real meaning of their efficacity *ex opere operato*, as our theologians express it. Once the meaning of *opus operatum* is rightly understood, it will be seen that it is simply the strict logic, applied to the facts, to living, of the doctrine, fundamental for Protestants themselves, that in salvation all is ultimately grace, a pure gift of God, a free gift of his generosity, unmerited and impossible to merit.

Yet Protestants will never come to recognise that this is what Catholic theology of the efficacity of the sacraments *ex opere operato* really means, if, in the actual conduct of Catholics, it seems that the sacramental rites mean to them nothing different from some kind of superstitious or magical practice.

Here it is evident that true 'ecumenicism' is a work in which the witness of the most ordinary of the faithful, the witness of their whole life, is of no less importance than the works of doctors, and even of the most solemn decisions of popes and Councils. In the years ahead, which will doubtless be so significant for the whole future of Christian unity, let us show our awareness of this, not only in what we think but above all in our whole way of acting.

Scripture conceived in a living community. The "community of interpretation" came first. Every man stands in a commun of interps.